Dogtags and Pearls 4

Lessons from Heaven

Katherine A. Sands

ISBN-9798549182547

DEDICATION

These writings would not have come about without the influence of my spiritual mother and mentor, Shirley Duckworth. Without her, I wouldn't be where I am today. She was God's gift to me at a time when I needed a godly role model. She listened to my immature ranting, prayed for me when I was crazy, put up with me and loved me, even when she didn't want to. She encouraged me to journal my relationship with God. I love her dearly and treasure the friendship we have. She is a serious Kingdom builder and influence in her family, an intercessor and a rare gem in the church. Her presence will be sorely missed when she graduates to Heaven to join the great cloud of witnesses. She is a true picture of Titus 2:3 and 4…how the older women are to teach the younger women in the church.

CONTENTS

Preface

This is my fourth book in the series of the Dogtags and Pearls, Lessons From Heaven books. I didn't plan this. I started writing on the blog...and then one book was published, and then two. At the time, I didn't know there would be any more, but it looks like they will continue to come out because I'm still writing at dogtagsandpearls.com. The title comes from the idea of dog tags as a rough and plain adornment, where pearls are considered of high value and precious. Never judge a book by its cover, my grandmother always said, and she wasn't talking about books. You never know what "pearls" something plain might contain, be it books or people!

The posts in this book were all written during this current year, 2021. They come through the filter of a year that so far, has been filled with strange, even bizarre happenings in our country. It appears the entire structure of our society is undergoing an upheaval of the type that threatens the safety and welfare of us all. That includes the governing authorities, the medical community, digital/social media, print media, retail and monetary industries, and elementary and higher education; nothing is exempt. All of the structures of society that Americans have come to rely upon appear to be coming apart at the seams. Laws are no longer upheld, but are for the most part totally ignored. Government, media and medical establishments all seek to censor voices so that only one narrative of events is allowed. The education sector seeks to do the same. Forced coercion into taking an experimental "vaccine," along with forced lockdown of society is happening all over the world. The waters we navigate are choppy indeed. The din of voices surges louder and louder as one group seeks to take control and another pushes back against it.

But there is still a God who watches events from Heaven, Who indeed knows what is happening and Who is still interested in his crowning creation....man.

My desire in these essays is to encourage the reader's faith and stimulate a desire to serve the One who died to save us as well as feed your spirit with biblical revelations. May God use my stories to do so. (Except where indicated, all scripture references are from the NKJV.)

Katherine Sands

1. Why Does The Storm Come?

I want to examine a phenomenon I see in the bible in a couple of places. There are probably more, but in the past few days I have been zeroing in on these two. The Holy Spirit has been speaking to me through them.

In Mark Chapter 4, Jesus told the disciples to get in a boat on the Sea of Galilee and "go to the other side." There was obviously a missionary intent and a job to do, which we shall see later. The disciples were in training, so even though the command may have sounded small and insignificant, the order to "go to the other side" was not small and insignificant. They were Jesus' words...the Jesus who said He "...only said what He heard the Father say...Selah (pause and think about that.)

So the word of God was SPOKEN aloud and the journey began. Jesus went to sleep. This fact never ceases to amaze me. He was asleep in the boat, fast asleep it would seem, because the storm started and He was still sleeping. The disciples became full of fear because of the storm and had to awaken Him. Of course, He rebuked them because He had given them a command and now they were reacting to the storm. They were backing down from the order He had given because circumstances made them afraid.

The "storms of life" define us. Will we make our decisions based on what we see with our natural eyes? Or will we stay focused on God's word, His command to us?

The storm came about for the purpose of hindering or stopping the plan that had been given to Jesus. It was to stop Him and the disciples from "going to the other side." It was to CHALLENGE the words that He spoke. It had a purpose. And when you continue reading to find out what happened when they arrived on the other side, you get an idea why the storm was so huge. (A man full of demons was delivered. That's a pretty big deal because after he was delivered, he then went and evangelized that area.)

I believe the "storm" we see today in our nation is very much related to words that God's people are speaking in their prayers. We are watching a spiritual clash between good and evil as prophets have been speaking words from Heaven. The "storm," or resistance, has come to challenge and to discourage believers from continuing their stand against the darkness.

Let's look at another example of a "storm" arising to defeat the plan of God. Paul in the Book of Acts, Chapter 27 embarked on a trip to Rome. He had been told by the Spirit of God that was the plan of God for him. Paul had confidence that he had heard correctly. But he also perceived that something would happen on that trip.

Paul was very well acquainted with the storms that accompany the word of God. He had experienced much resistance in his life as preached the gospel to the Jews. He warned the captain and crew of the ship that trouble lay ahead, but they ignored him. After the typhoon storm hit, it seemed that all would be lost.

An angel arrived to give Paul instructions, which Paul conveyed to the captain and the men. They were pretty desperate, so they agreed to do as Paul said. He told them to eat and then throw everything else overboard to lighten the load. He also told them the ship would be lost, but all their lives would be spared, which is exactly what happened. They shipwrecked on an island, a detour because men would not listen. Paul's knowledge of the plan of God helped him to hold on to faith. He knew what was ahead. He knew this was not the end because he was due to go before Caesar Rome.

Fast forward to today...we are seeing an immense storm that threatens to swallow our republic and its people. Take courage, this is only the storm sent to destroy your confidence and cause you to fear. Refuse both. Take comfort that God is only good and that His plans are good for you and for the country. Read His word and you will find the comfort you need. His word is true; it cannot lie. Listen to His word, speak His word aloud and you will find peace and rest for your soul. We were created by Him and He cares for us more than we know. Trust His plan even if you don't quite know how it will all work out. That's what Paul did.

Dear Jesus, Storms are tough on us humans. We live so much by what we taste, see, feel and think, more than we live by Your eternal truth. For most of us, the storms may be sickness, children in trouble, financial worries, lack of things we need and currently, we are watching our country and our political leaders in turbulence and confusion. I turn to You as my source of peace and comfort in the midst of all the storms. "WHENEVER I AM AFRAID, I WILL TRUST IN YOU." Psalm 56:3 I worship and praise You for Your great love and protection for me and those I care for. Thank You for all that You have done, are doing and will do in the future. Bless our country and our people. ~~ January 16, 2021

NOTES

2. Moses Challenges a World Ruler...And How That Worked Out

Moses was living in the wilderness of Midian when God approached him and commissioned him to go and challenge Pharaoh of Egypt and tell him to release God's people to go worship in the wilderness. Moses had fled to the wilderness after his first effort to save his brethren from the cruelty of Pharaoh had failed. He fled Egypt just 40 years prior, after killing an Egyptian. You see, he really was called to deliver his brethren from their slavery to the Egyptians. (Acts 7:19-29) That **was** the plan of God for his life. He just blew it the first time he tried. He wasn't ready and it wasn't time. He tried to do it in his own strength and not in God's strength. Moses had much to learn about God.

I think we all do that. We sense something of God's call on our life and we act on it. We have inspiration to do it. We have abilities and talent. We may feel compelled. But it's premature and things don't work out. But that doesn't mean it's over...

So Moses went to Egypt and challenged the world ruler of that time. Think about that. He was 80 years old! He only had a wooden staff in his hands and he went to the most powerful man in the world, and demanded he let a few million slaves have some days off work to go and worship in the wilderness.

I'm sure Pharaoh laughed. The whole court probably laughed at this sheepherder from the wilderness. And then, to reward the Israelites for Moses's audacity, he made their labor even harder. They usually made bricks using straw, but Pharaoh punished them and took their straw away. They were still expected to keep their quotas the same. I don't know much about brick making, but I would assume that the straw probably helped the bricks hold together.

The Israelites really didn't enjoy having their work made more difficult, so of course they got mad at Moses and blamed him for their predicament. We would too.

So things were getting tough for them, and they weren't really sure about this deliverance thing and going on a camping trip in the desert to worship a God they probably didn't know much about, except maybe through stories. They had been in Egypt for over 400 years and slaves for much of that time. They didn't know much else besides that. But the time of the promise had drawn near. See Acts 7:6,7 and Acts 7:17.

A prophetic man named Bill Cloud said something about this particular story that I have never forgotten. He said, "The things we think are bad, God says are good."

If you believe in the scripture from Romans 8:28 that says, "AND WE KNOW THAT ALL THINGS WORK TOGETHER FOR GOOD FOR THOSE WHO LOVE GOD AND ARE CALLED ACCORDING TO HIS PURPOSE," you know what that means.

If you know the bible story, you know there were 10 judgments that came upon the whole nation of Egypt because Pharaoh refused to let the people of God leave to worship their God. The interesting thing about all of that is, while Egypt and Pharaoh were being dealt with, the Israelites, it is said, were not touched by the judgments. They dwelt "in the secret place of the Almighty God," kept safe from the terrible judgments that came upon the place.

The judgments went from bad to worse. One of them was complete darkness over Egypt, "BUT ALL THE CHILDREN

OF ISRAEL HAD LIGHT IN THEIR DWELLINGS." Exodus 10:23 Goshen, where the Israelites lived, was the "suburb." Since they were slaves, it may have been more like an 'inner city" or a slum. But they had light while, in the rest of the country, there was a total blackout. Do you think the Egyptians would have wanted to have some friends in Goshen? I do! Think about your own county. If the whole rest of the nation was in a blackout and your county had light, wouldn't everyone want to come to your county? I think they would.

This all looks bad, right? It certainly looks bad for Egypt, or can we call them, the people who don't believe in God? But God's people were doing all right; they were being protected from what the Egyptians were going through. It was all leading up to something. This was a mighty display of a power greater than the world ruling power of that time. A lot of the Egyptians were convinced too, because we later find them leaving Egypt right along with the Israelites. They saw there was favor on them and, I would submit to you, that they believed in their God.

600,000 men, along with women and children, left Egypt and headed out to an unknown future. But God was leading them. They took a huge leap of faith. The difficulties of their slavery pressed on them until they were ready, perhaps even eager, to leave. The plagues that came upon Egypt caused the Egyptians to want them to leave! They gave the Israelites all their gold and jewelry to take with them. Maybe they were paying them to leave town.

So what the Israelites thought was bad, actually worked in their favor: it pushed them to leave Egypt. It made them more willing. This was to fulfill a promise to their forefather, Abraham. God had told him the nation would be in Egypt 400 years. Genesis 15:13,14. It was now time to go.

"Now the sojourning of the children of Israel, who dwelt in Egypt, was four hundred and thirty years. And it came to pass at the end of the four hundred and thirty years, even the self-same day it came to pass, that all the hosts of the Lord went out from the land of Egypt." Exodus 12:40-41

I think God may work like this a lot. He stirs us, making us dissatisfied with where we are spiritually, and in our everyday circumstances. He may allow discomfort to come into our lives, not physical discomfort per se, but perhaps some type of hardship. This is designed to make us change in some fashion, to press us towards Him. It will work for our good, no matter what it is. We must keep faith!

If you know the story, you will remember that after they left, and with many Egyptians with them, then Pharaoh changed his mind about letting all those slaves leave. He and his army in chariots chased them down to the Red Sea. The Israelites were hemmed in between the Egyptians and the Red Sea, but the people saw a miraculous deliverance of God that day, not only in delivering them from the Egyptians, but destroying their enemy also. Moses had told them they would never see the Egyptians again. It was quite a day...

Read the whole story of their miraculous deliverance in Exodus 14. ~~January 28, 2021

NOTES

3. When It Looks Like It's Not Going to Happen, Part 1

As of this writing, conservatives are reeling, at least a bit and some maybe a lot, at the apparent loss of the Presidency to Joe Biden in our country. There's a lot that could be said about that, but at the moment I'm thinking of a couple of bible stories…

The first one I'm thinking of is King David. But I'm thinking of the time BEFORE he was accepted as king. I'm thinking of the time when he had officially been anointed and chosen as king, but he wasn't on the throne yet…in fact…

King Saul was in the position of power in Israel in 1 Kings and Saul disobeyed God. He was told by the prophet that the kingdom would be taken from his leadership. This put him in a sour mood, so David the shepherd boy, was brought in to play music for him, to soothe his frayed nerves. There came a time that Saul became jealous of David after David had taken on the giant Goliath and won. Apparently, songs in that time period were stories, and the people sang songs that Saul had slain his thousands, and David his tens of thousands." This made Saul, well…grumpy, to say the least. This is what insecurity breeds. When a person is insecure, they can only compare themselves with others and be jealous. They are unable to rejoice and be glad for someone who has something they themselves want. Saul was out of favor with God and was going to be replaced. The prophet's words had foretold it. Saul had done some very stupid things. One thing was trying to kill David. Now remember, David had already been told that he would be king. He wasn't told when it would happen. I would submit he actually had no idea when it would happen, because it certainly didn't LOOK as if things were moving in that direction. David was forced to flee Saul's presence and go into hiding, living in the woods and in caves. There were men who joined with David and left the "establishment" king.

There were battles, even in hiding, but David insisted on keeping his heart right towards Saul, who was actually his father-in-law. Remember that Saul had given David his daughter as a wife as a reward for killing Goliath. Once, when Saul happened to lie down and sleep in the cave where David was hiding, David was prodded by one of the men who said "God has put Saul in your hands." The most that David could do was cut off a piece of Saul's tunic, but his heart bothered him about even doing that.

Saul, in his madness, eventually met a violent end, but that still didn't put David on the throne. Those who followed Saul wanted to keep the throne and set one of Saul's heirs as king. Eventually, those who had followed Saul recognized and accepted David as their king too. And so, the nation was reunited with the warrior King David in the position that the prophet had foretold he would occupy.

David had many chances to give up, in despair and gloom and pessimism. And there were several times he may have done it for a time. At one point in the wilderness, after a group of marauders had ran off with everyone's wives and children, his own men were at the point of stoning David. But David prayed. Will we give up when things don't go the way we think they should?

Romans 8:28 says that ALL things work together for the good for those who love God and are called according to His purpose. Even the delay, the resistance, the dark days work together for our good. Believing that is the only way we can push through those times. As long as we live on this earth, we will experience opposition because there is a devil that hates us and he is on the loose in this world. God does not bring us evil, but we are allowed to experience the opposition to build up our faith. If I don't exercise my muscles, they will become weak and flabby. It's the same way with our faith. We need that resistance to stay strong in faith. Exercising it is the only way to keep it that way!

Dear Jesus, Help us today to understand Your ways and Your plan for our lives. Open our eyes to see Your workings more and more. We lean on You for everything and thank and praise You for all You have done for us. ~~February 16, 2021

NOTES

4. When It Looks Like It's Not Going to Happen, Part 2

There's another story I find interesting too, about when things don't go the way we think they should. I am reminded of a story where the nation of Israel had to pass a severe judgment on one of their relative tribes....

The story is in the book of Judges, chapters 19 and 20. A little backstory...a priest went to get his concubine who had left him. We don't know if he was a mean man or not, but as you will see in a bit, one might wonder. At least I do. The concubine was living at her father's house and the priest went there to pick her up. They went on their way back home and passed into a land inhabited by the Benjamites. Benjamin was one of the 12 sons of Jacob, so these were cousins. But some of the Benjamites had sunk to a very sinful low place. The priest and his concubine were invited to spend the night in a man's house. That night, a group of Benjamites started pounding on the door demanding that the owner of the house give them the male visitor. The host was so horrified that they would demand that of him, he offered his own daughter to them. The priest then pushed his concubine out there instead to the men and they had their way with her all night. There are no details given on this, but it was not good. Apparently, she found her way back to the house sometime in the night, but died on the doorstep of the home. When the priest opened the door in the morning, he found her there and tried to waken her, but she was dead. He was so horrified that they killed his concubine; he cut her into 12 pieces and sent a piece to each tribe, asking for justice. (I am not going to discuss his actions however, because that is not the main point of what I'm pointing out here, but I do question his behavior too.)

So the tribes of Israel convened; they knew they had to do something. This was a sin so grievous, it had to be dealt with. My guess is they may have known it was happening all along and let it go on and on, until this event happened and they could no longer ignore it. There just comes a time…the priest was demanding justice. The first thing they did was ask the Benjamites to hand over the ones who had done this horrible thing. But as can be customary in families, the whole tribe refused to turn over their relatives. Even if they were a group of criminals, they would be protected from the consequences of their deeds. What could have been punishment for just a few ended up becoming a judgment on the whole tribe.

The cousin tribes prayed, and God told them to go after the Benjamites. They did and lost 22,000 of their own men in the first engagement. That's a lot of men! So they went back to God and again He said, go after them. They did and lost 18,000 more the next day. Following God's instructions didn't seem to be working out very well…

They went back to God again, this time in fasting and weeping for the losses they had taken. They were truly broken. And God once again told them to go after the Benjamites, and this time, He told them they would win. And they did win. In the process, the eleven other tribes wiped out all but 600 men of the tribe of Benjamin. The whole tribe was gone except for them. This grieved the cousin tribes a great deal, but they had taken great losses also. Dealing with sin brings grief to all involved, and especially if it's in your own family.

This story reminds me of how sometimes, we try and try again, and we fail. After awhile, we don't want to try anymore, because by then, we are conditioned that we most likely will fail. We desperately need a word and a promise from God to continue on! We need to know that our cause is righteous. We need to know that He is with us.

The nation knew they were supposed to do this, but failure kept happening and lives were being lost in this massive battle against sin. Fasting seems to be the added element in this story that brought the needed victory. (In the New Testament, we see Jesus adding fasting to a situation also when he said "This kind doesn't come out except for prayer and fasting," when his disciples were unable to cast out a demon.) There are times that we must keep persevering in a matter until we see the victory. We need to pay attention to what God will speak to us. He knows how we can get the victory.

The Israelites could have given up after the first 22,000 were killed. They could have given up after the second day of battle when thousands more of their own died. Remember that both days, God had told them to go into battle. Just because God leads us to do something may not mean we see an instant win; we may suffer hurt. In my early days of becoming a Christ follower, there were battles I did not think I could win. My spiritual enemy was very strong, but God kept encouraging me through His word and I eventually saw victory in a major sin area of my life.

The Benjamites must have been ferocious warriors to inflict this kind of damage. Of course we know they wanted to protect their relatives, but whether they knew it or not, they were also protecting a lifestyle of sin; perhaps they even had some agreement with it. (I would submit that demonic powers can make people stronger than they would normally be. I have heard stories of great strength in unlikely people that may only be explained in that way.)

Be encouraged; whatever God has called you to do, He has also equipped you to do. He will provide everything you need to get through it. There is always resistance to whatever God is calling us to. We must keep the faith! And I personally am grateful I don't have to go out and whack people with a sword, praise the Lord! ~~February 16, 2021

NOTES

5. God's Plans Delayed?

Can God's plan be delayed? Does man determine when things happen? Does God get frustrated when man doesn't "follow the plan"?

Well, I guess we should start in the Garden of Eden, when Adam and Eve didn't follow the plan. They decided to make their own decision, apart from God's instructions, and we see how that worked out. We have to know that God already knew it was going to happen (because He knows everything) and had already made preparation for the remedy, "*...the Lamb, slain from the foundation of the world,*" (Rev. 13:8) gives us a hint that that is true.

We see the Israelites in the wilderness and God told them they could have the Promised Land; He had **already** given it to them. Twelve spies went to check everything out; two came back, saying, "yes we can do it, they are bread for us." Ten came back and said, oh man those people are giants and we are grasshoppers. (my paraphrase) The ten spread their fear and doubt among the people, who then refused to obey out of fear. So the plan was delayed for 40 years while that first generation died out and their kids got prepared to do it.

There are all kinds of examples where man did not do as he was asked and it put a delay on what God was wanting. Keep in mind that God already knows all of this, what men will do or not do.

Lately it has been brought to my attention about what happened to the Apostle Paul in Acts 27. Paul knew that God was sending him to Rome. However Paul perceived that the ship that he was getting on was going to meet an ill fate with loss of life and cargo. The men in charge ignored him and embarked on the journey anyway. A major typhoon storm called a Euroclydon came upon them for several days and it seemed the ship would be lost. But Paul announced to the crew that an angel had appeared to him and told him the ship would be lost, but all the men on the ship would be saved, which is exactly what happened.

The ship ran aground on an island and all the men made it to shore. They met some natives and Paul preached the gospel to them and healed their people. A viper bit him and attempted to take him out, but that didn't work either. Then another ship arrived to pick them all up and take them on to Rome. Paul was destined for Rome…that was the plan of God, even though unbelieving men managed to delay things for a while.

Jonah is another prophet of God who disobeyed, and by that action, put many men's lives in danger. When he was dealt with and turned and obeyed God, he saw the repentance of probably the largest, most evil city of that time. See, God cared about them too. And that city of Nineveh actually survived for another 100 years before judgment eventually came.

Man's disobedience can delay the plan of God, but it seems not for forever. All things still work together for the good of those who love God and are called according to His purpose. Romans 8:28

Personally I'm all for getting it right the first time if at all possible. I want to hear *"Well done, thou good and faithful servant"* when I see Him face to face. ~~ February 16, 2021

NOTES

6. Our God Endured Torture For Us

I love patterns that show up in the bible...patterns can confirm things you thought you noticed. When it comes along twice, I really start paying attention. God paints pictures through the Old Testament bible stories. As we study them, we can see spiritual lessons emerge.

For example, in the Old Testament, a lamb was slaughtered each year for the sins of the people. The lamb was killed mercifully, by slitting its throat. The lamb's blood was shed for the sins of all the people one time during the year, but the lamb's death was not fully able to take away those sins; it could only cover them. Other animals were also used as sin offerings during the year for personal sin. But on the Day of Atonement that happened once a year, a lamb was used to make atonement for the nation. This lamb foreshadowed the real Lamb (Jesus) Who was coming.

Hebrews 10:1-4 "For the law, having a shadow of the good things to come, and not the very image of the things, can never with these same sacrifices, which they offer continually year by year, make those who approach perfect. For then would they not have ceased to be offered? For the worshippers, once purified, would have had no more consciousness of sins. But in those sacrifices there is a reminder of sins every year. For it is not possible that the blood of bulls and goats could take away sins."

Jesus endured much more than a quick merciful death like the Old Testament lamb received. Jesus CHOSE to endure torture before His death. He was beaten and whipped until the skin on his back was broken open. The Passion of the Christ movie graphically brought this aspect out. The cruelty was more than I could even watch. This torture, this whipping, was for the healing of our bodies. In the picture of the actual lamb being slain for our sins, a somewhat more merciful death was seen, although Isaiah speaks of a man whose "visage was marred more than any man." (Is. 52.14) He was the Lamb slain before the foundation of the world. Our God went through much more to purchase our salvation to the very fullest. He gave it all. These are things to ponder...

Jesus's death fulfilled what that allegorical symbolic lamb did. His sacrifice, though, completely removed sins, past, present, and future. His sacrifice cleansed the conscience.

The thing that impacted me from the movie, "The Passion of the Christ," was how determined Jesus was to make it to the cross. That was the main picture I walked away with. The flogging and cruel beating was so horrific, it seemed like He could not make it there, as He fell and seemed unable to continue...but He did make it there. I think He knew He had to. Without the cross, the salvation of men could not happen...He knows we are but dust. The book of Hebrews says, "*for the joy set before Him, He endured the cross.*" I believe the joy was in knowing His created human beings would be saved from eternal damnation and spend eternity with Him.

Scripture says that by rising from the dead, Jesus made an open show of the devil. Colossians 2:15 "*Having disarmed principalities and powers, He made a public spectacle of them, triumphing over them in it."*

The devil illegally killed an innocent man. That is why Jesus could not be held in death. He was condemned by men, but loved by God. He had no sin and was innocent. Killing him was illegal. But He took our place, our punishment, by His own choice. It truly is a remarkable story of love...how God sent a baby to earth to be the salvation of man, to live as a man, and grow up among men. He was sent from God to tell mankind He was the savior, with signs and wonders accompanying (the same signs that His church is supposed to be displaying, by the way)

Receive His love today! It is real and it is amazing. ~~March 8, 2021

NOTES

7. The Way God Does Things Is Not The Way We Do Them

In Judges 6, we see the Israelites under severe oppression by a group of people called the Midianites. The oppression was so bad, these Midianites would come and steal the crops from the fields before the Israelites could get to them. This caused a severe food shortage for the people. (This reminds me of how the Soviet Union took all the food grown in Ukraine many years ago and the Ukranians starved by the thousands.)

A man named Gideon was hiding out protecting the wheat he was threshing. That day, as Gideon pondered the stories of miracles he had heard that God had done for his forefathers, he wondered where that God was and why his generation didn't see any miracles. God responded by calling Gideon to the task of confronting the Midianites. Gideon couldn't believe that God was really calling him to this and, after some back and forth conversation and a visit by an angel, and a couple of "fleeces," Gideon grew in faith and courage. He became convinced that God was with him and that God wanted to rescue the nation.

Gideon managed to assemble 32,000 men who would fight alongside him. The people were tired of being bullied by the Midianites. But God said 32,000 was too many. What?

Judges 7:2 "*The people who are with you are too many for Me to give the Midianites into their hands, lest Israel claim glory for itself against Me, saying, 'My own hand has saved me.' Now therefore, proclaim in the hearing of the people, saying, 'Whoever is fearful and afraid, let him turn and depart at once from Mount Gilead.'* " And twenty-two thousand of the people returned, and ten thousand remained. The 22,000 were afraid of going up against the Midianites...they had to leave.

Too many? Really? Well, they just lost about 2/3 of their number. The story says the Midianites' numbers could not be counted, there was so many, as we shall see. And Gideon has just 10,000 men...and that group is about to get pared down to only 300 men....what?

I feel like that's where we are in our country right now. Those who are afraid are being outed. Our leaders are afraid of the bullying that they suffer at the hands of those who want to take over and oppress the citizens of the United States. The bullying continues and even gets worse, but they are all still afraid. They may be afraid for their lives, because the bullies are violent and WILL harm those who oppose them.

Judges 7:12 "*Now the Midianites and Amalekites, all the people of the East, were lying in the valley as numerous as locusts; and their camels were without number, as the sand by the seashore in multitude.*"

But I say, at what point do those who are being bullied turn and knock the bully out? How much are those being bullied expected to take? This is like in school when the bully hits you in the chest, and you back up, then he hits you again, and you back up. At what point do you decide to defend yourself?

How much will you take? How much will WE take as the bullies rule and reign over the "school yard" of the United States?

It looked really bad for Gideon and the Israelites. But God had a plan. God is always in the business of defeating the many with the few. This is an amazing story. 300 brave men were chosen for Gideon's army, and in the end, the enemy armies destroyed each other and Israel was delivered from their oppressors. Gideon (or maybe God) managed to convince the enemy that Gideon was a scary guy, and in the confusion of it all, they turned on each other! Might we see the same thing here in America?

I believe God has a plan. Remember...the heavenly armies we can't see are greater than the ones we can see. And if God be for us, who can be against us! Be strong and courageous, for the Lord your God is with you!

Lord, we declare that there is no answer for the problems in our nation apart from You. You are all there is. We take our place and wait for Your instructions. We know that with You and the angels of Heaven, we are a majority. We declare that Your promises are true and the evil one and all his plans are defeated! In Jesus's mighty name. We trust You only, Jesus. ~~March 16, 2021

NOTES

8. Who Are God's Friends?

"This is My commandment, that you love one another as I have loved you. Greater love has no one than this, than to lay down one's life for his friends. You are My friends if you do whatever I command you. No longer do I call you servants, for a servant does not know what his master is doing; but I have called you friends, for all things that I heard from My Father I have made known to you. You did not choose Me, but I chose you and appointed you that you should go and bear fruit..."

Jesus said this to His disciples in John 15:12-16, but being a friend of God is an option that is open to all men. There are special characteristics of those who would be God's friends. "You are my friends if you do whatever I command you." So according to this passage, a friend of God would be a person who is obedient to God, who trusts Him enough to follow His directions.

Jesus said, "I have called you friends, for all things that I heard from My Father I have made known to you." Jesus told His disciples things that He didn't tell other people. May I submit to you that if you are a friend of God, you will be a disciple, a follower? If we look at the picture portrayed in the New Testament of a disciple, it is a person who spends a lot of time with God in order to know Him, to learn from Him. We see this same characteristic in the life of Joshua in the Old

Testament, of whom it was said, he never left the tent of meeting when Moses was alive. Joshua went on to become the next leader of the Israelites who took the promises of God to heart and went into the Promised Land to claim what God had promised was his. Ex 33:11

There were a select few disciples who lived and traveled with Jesus constantly. After Jesus told a parable to the people, we read that the disciples would take Jesus aside and ask Him what it meant. They always sought to understand and to ask Him questions. Jesus had said to them, it had been given to them to know the mysteries of the Kingdom of God, but to those who were on the outside, He spoke in parables, ...Mark 4:11-12 When the disciples asked for the explanation, Jesus would tell them. Where were the other people? Obviously they were not drawing near to the Him to find answers and get understanding. The book of Proverbs says we must get wisdom and understanding. Proverbs 4:7

I have met a few people in my life who take issue with asking God questions. But we never see Jesus chastising his disciples when they asked questions. He told them it was given to them to know the secrets of the Kingdom. He encouraged them. I have always asked God questions after I got filled with the Spirit. And God has just about always given me the answers to my questions with insight into most things. You cannot tell me that I should not question God. We read of Abraham having a Q&A with God in the matter of Sodom and Gomorrah. After God told Abraham what He was going to do with Sodom and Gomorrah, Abraham tried to save his nephew Lot by repeatedly asking God how many righteous would it take to stop the destruction of those cities.

I believe that, just like the disciples in the bible, a disciple always asks questions. Those who do not ask will not receive understanding. God does not hand out information casually. What would be the point of telling someone something they do not value? Mark 4:12 goes on to say about those who are given parables..."*That seeing they may see, and not perceive; and hearing they may hear, and not understand; lest at any time they should be converted, and their sins should be forgiven them.*" The parables are designed to separate those who desire to learn about the Kingdom and those who do not. It's like He gives you a hint, a picture, a clue, and in order to know more, you must draw near and ask for more. But He's not going to give all the secrets away to the casual listener. It's a matter of VALUE. What do you value? The disciple, the studious, those who are interested are who He will reveal things to.

God desires all men to be saved and come to the knowledge of the truth. 1 Timothy 2:4. But not all men do get saved. Salvation is available to all, and some are content with just having that assurance, but a disciple is not content with just salvation...they must have more knowledge of God. They desire to know about the Kingdom.

We are to seek, ask and knock, according to Matthew 7:7. The promise is if we seek, we shall find, if we ask, it will be given to us, and if we knock, the door will be opened to us. James 1:5 says, *"If anyone lacks wisdom, let him ask of God,"* so yes we are to ask Him for answers. He has plans for our lives. How will we find what those plans are if we do not ask? ~~March 16, 2021

NOTES

9. Psalm 103: A Prayer

I find Psalm 103 to be so rich and full of the blessings of the Lord that I want in my life. David wrote this Psalm and it is a praise for the Lord's mercies. I like to pray it out loud to the Lord directly, such as in this manner, adding some of my own prayer inspiration (one can also say "I" instead of "we"):

"We bless You Lord and all that is within us, "We bless you and do not forget even one of Your benefits. We bless Your Holy Name.

"You have forgiven all of our sins, you have washed us clean and made us to stand in your very own righteousness by taking our sin upon yourself. You have paid for all of our guilt.

"You have healed all our diseases. You have delivered us from the dominion of darkness so that we might experience Your life.

"You have redeemed our lives from destruction, the destruction that satan had planned for the human race and for our lives too. We are redeemed from that. We are delivered and rescued from that destruction.

"You crown us with loving-kindness and tender mercies,

"You have satisfied my mouth with good things, both in eating good food and in tasting of Your word, and because you have satisfied my mouth with these good things, my youth is renewed day by day like the eagles. I shall have strength in my older years even as I did as a young person. I have tasted the powers of the age to come and seen that You are good. (Hebrews 6:5, Psalm 34:8)

"You execute righteousness and justice for all who are oppressed.

"You made known Your ways to Moses, Your acts to the children of Israel. You are merciful and gracious, slow to anger, and abounding in mercy.

"You will not always strive with us, nor will You keep Your anger forever (which has now been appeased through the sacrifice of Your Son). You have not dealt with us according to our sins, nor punished us according to our iniquities.

"For as the heavens are high above the earth, so great is Your mercy toward us who fear You; as far as the east is from the west, so far have You removed our transgressions from us.

"As a father pities his children, so You pity those who fear You. For You know our frame; You remember that we are dust.

"As for man, our days are like grass; as a flower of the field, so we flourish. For the wind passes over it, and it is gone, And its place remembers it no more.

"But Your mercy is from everlasting to everlasting on those who fear You And Your righteousness to children's children,

To such as keep Your covenant, And to those who remember Your commandments to do them.

"You have established Your throne in Heaven And Your kingdom rules over all.

"Bless the Lord, you His angels, who excel in strength, who do His word, heeding the voice of His word.

"Bless the Lord, all you His hosts, You ministers of His, who do His pleasure.

"Bless the Lord, all His works, In all places of His dominion.

"Bless the Lord, O my soul!"

Psalms 25 and 91 are equally good for praying in this manner. I have prayed this way for many years and have found it very helpful for building my faith in the goodness, mercy, and protection of God.~~March 23, 2021

NOTES

10. Worship: Your Way to Victory

"But we all, with unveiled face, beholding as in a mirror the glory of the Lord, are being transformed into the same image from glory to glory, just as by the Spirit of the Lord." 2 Corinthians 3:18

How do we behold the Lord? We worship Him. We express our gratitude to Him. When we read His word, we are beholding His glory. We read of what He has done. He is our Creator. He is great, He is magnificent, He is love. He loves us. We owe our existence to Him. He planned for each one of us to come to be on this earth with a plan for the course of our lives. (Jeremiah 1:5, Psalm 139:16)

If I was going to teach a new believer what to do first, I think I would start with worship. If you want to really know God, learn to worship Him. You will behold His image (spiritually) as you worship Him and the scriptures says, you will be transformed! So how do we worship God? Is it just singing songs to Him? Is it praying? What exactly is worship?

Let's look at some examples from the bible to get an idea of what worshipping God might be like and what it does for us. The bible is the instruction manual. The answer to every question is in that book. In the beginning of man's history, Adam and Eve were placed in the garden. The garden was perfect. There were no problems; it was a paradise. Everything was supplied for them and they had no worries. Adam and Eve talked with God in the cool of the day, the scriptures say. There was no devil. The pair were supposed to tend the garden and could freely talk to God and He to them. There was only one thing that God asked them not to do, and we know what happened there and that changed everything. But as long as they walked and talked with God, everything was good.

After Adam gave his dominion over to satan when he was tempted, things changed. Animal sacrifices began in order for man to have relationship with God. We see this in the animal coverings that God made for them to cover their nakedness. We briefly see their children, Abel and Cain, make sacrifices and worship the God of their parents after they had been driven from the garden to live in the world where man no longer had dominion. He was now a slave to satan. Everything was difficult, but God was still involved in their lives. Genesis, Chapter 4.

Joshua, the successor to Moses, spent all of his time learning from Moses and stayed in the presence of the Lord in Moses's tent. He was eventually chosen to lead the Israelites into the Promised Land. Exodus 33:11

King David spent a lot of time worshipping out on the hill by himself while tending his father's sheep. David was a worshipper and because of that, he had the courage to challenge the giant Goliath. When David worshipped, he was built up on the inside as he worshipped and listened to God. David had the courage to kill a lion and a bear when they threatened his sheep. David found victory when he worshipped God. 1 Samuel 17.

King Jehoshaphat put the praise team out in front of his army when he was surrounded by foreign armies that were coming to destroy him. Who would do that? But that is what God told him to do to obtain victory over their enemies. He was told, "You will not have to fight today, for the Lord will fight for you." 2 Chronicles 16

Most of the Psalms are written records of King David's prayers and worship to God. Some are written by other worshippers. The heart of a worshipper is seen in the Psalms. Start there to experience God's presence. Read the Psalms aloud. It is helpful for your heart to hear those words. It builds faith. They can become your prayers too. Psalm 150 speaks of praising and worshipping the Lord. Worship should be a major part of a believer's relationship with God as patterned in the scriptures. In the book of Revelations, we find worship going on in Heaven.

I promise you, you will find victory when you worship Him. He will empower you. ~~April 4, 2021

NOTES

11. Are Bible Stories Still Relevant to Our Lives?

Why do I write about the great men and women of faith in the Bible? Why do I examine their stories and and point out what they did and how they lived?

2 Tim 3:16 says, "*All Scripture is given by inspiration of God, and is profitable for doctrine, for reproof, for correction, for instruction in righteousness,*

Hebrews 6:12 says see to it...."*that you do not become sluggish, but imitate those who through faith and patience inherit the promises.*"

Hebrews, Chapter 11 is called the Hall of Faith by some Christians. It is a short chronology of those of faith from the past and lists the feats they accomplished. If we can learn from the lives of those who have gone before, perhaps we might not make the same mistakes, right?

1 Corinthians 10:11 speaks of Israel in the wilderness in this manner: "*Now these things happened to them as an example, and they were written for our instruction, upon whom the ends of the ages have come.*"

The Bible was recorded and kept not only as an historical record of the works of God in the world, but is also meant for our instruction! We would do well to heed what it says. It has all of the answers to life.

Our father in the faith, Abraham, left his homeland, not knowing where he was going, and waited many years to finally father a son when he was about 100 years old and Sarah was 90. From Abraham, all the nations of the earth are blessed because of his faith and example.

We see the faith of Joseph, who endured betrayal by his brothers, going into captivity and being imprisoned. He was finally exalted to second in command in Egypt after interpreting Pharaoh's dreams and advising him of the solution, thereby saving his own people and many others from starvation during the famine.

There's the faith of Moses, who had probably given up on his dream to rescue his brethren, but answered the call when God spoke to him forty years later. Moses went on to challenge the ruler of Egypt, executed judgment on Egypt's gods, and rescued the nation from their slavery, leading them through the Red Sea, while Egypt was destroyed.

We read of the faith of Gideon, who, with a 300 man army whittled down from 32,000, went up against armies too many to number and won freedom for Israel from the oppression of the Midianites. Imagine that.

We see the faith of David who was anointed as king, but patiently waited for God to exalt him, living in the wilderness and in caves. David killed the Philistine giant, Goliath, when he was a teenager because he had faith and hated seeing his nation quaking in fear at Goliath's threats. David wrote many of the Psalms out of his relationship with God.

There's the faith of Elijah, who spearheaded revival in Israel by challenging the false god Baal to a demonstration of power and then killed 850 prophets of Baal under the cruel reign of Ahab and Jezebel. He declared the beginning of a famine and when it would end. He ate food brought by ravens in the famine and raised a dead boy to life.

We read of the faith of Esther, a young Jewish maiden who married a heathen king, then risked her very life to save her people from extinction when they were threatened by the wicked, conniving Haman.

We see the faith of the prophet Daniel taken into captivity as a young man, his name and language taken from him; he was made a eunuch to serve in the palace, submitting to several ungodly kings in Babylon. He was thrown in a lion's den for a night, and survived. But Daniel was faithful to God and received great revelations of what would come in the end times. He was visited by angels who brought the prophetic words. He saw the end of the Babylonian captivity in the scriptures and prayed in agreement with God for it to come to pass.

These people did amazing, astonishing feats of faith all before Jesus came. The nation of Israel preserved these stories of faith in the Old Testament for us on whom the end of the ages has come. They are just some of our examples. They are pictures to help us live our lives by faith and assuredly are in the great cloud of witnesses spoken of in Hebrews 12 who are cheering us on in our race to be all and do all that God would have us do in these days. They are heroes, in my book.

Hebrews 11:1-2 "*Now faith is the substance of things hoped for, the evidence of things not seen. For by it the elders obtained a good testimony.*"~~April 17, 2021

NOTES

12. The Big Picture, Part 1

So what's the big picture story of man from the beginning of time? Who is man and why is he here on the earth? What is his purpose? Who is God and where does He fit into all of this?

God created the earth and everything in it. Genesis, Chapter 1. God is Creator and the originator of everything.

God said "Let us make man in Our image (the image of God), according to Our likeness; let them have dominion over the fish of the sea, over the birds of the air, and over the cattle, over all the earth and over every creeping thing that creeps on the earth." Genesis 1:26 So we are shown the plurality of the one God in this verse.

Then God blessed the man, and said, "Be fruitful and multiply; fill the earth and subdue it; have dominion over the fish of the sea, over the birds of the air, and over every living thing that moves on the earth."

That right there is PURPOSE. Gen. 2:15 Then the Lord God took the man and put him in the Garden of Eden to tend and keep it." There is the work that man was to do. Man needs purpose and man needs work.

This original commission of man has never changed. God has never gone back on His word regarding man's original purpose. Man was supposed to perform this purpose of rulership by submitting to the headship of God. But man messed up, so God had a plan on how to fix things. That plan was Jesus Christ, God's Son, who would come to earth as a man, just like Adam, and show man what he was supposed to be doing, show him how to take dominion legally, how to rule over sin and satan. Then He would die to redeem and restore man to his rightful place. Adam was supposed to deal with the devil in that first confrontation. Because he did not submit to God and resist the devil so as to make him flee (James 4:7), the future of the human race was to be born into a world where the devil reigned through sin, but…when Jesus, actually called the second or last Adam (1 Cor. 15:45), came…

Jesus deliberately took on Himself all the sins of man and died on the cross, even though He pleaded with the Father, "if there is any other way". (But there wasn't) This was the only way to bring man back to his rightful position in the plan of God, to restore man to his rightful place of legal authority in the earth, and to give him dominion over everything that Adam had lost, which included the devil and his cohorts who seek to destroy everything on the earth. That's just the beginning of redemption. We must go on from there and exercise this rulership.

The people of God who understand this are engaged in participating in this dominion position given back to them by Jesus Christ. "The earth He has given to the children of men." Psalms 115:16 They do this through prayer, which is actually hearing information from God and then speaking it back to God, giving agreement with the will of God in the earth. "Thy Kingdom come, thy will be done, on earth as it is in Heaven." We want the will of God in the earth, don't we? We don't want evil works to prevail. Well, God doesn't either…so there's two in agreement! And God is definitely a Winner! We also have fellowship with God by just talking to Him. There are several aspects to the word prayer.

That's the big picture.

The rest of the Bible is the story of God working to bring man back into that position of dominion. All judgment of the human race has now been committed to Jesus, who is waiting until the earth is made His footstool and all rebellion is put down. (Hebrews 10:13) That's where we come in. Jesus is looking for a bride to rule and reign with Him. We are that bride. One could say He is the sheriff and we are the deputies. We enforce what He tells us to enforce.

When everything is put under His feet and all things are in subjection to Him, then He will turn the Kingdom over to the Father, (1 Cor. 15:24) but until then, Jesus is the Head of it all. He is the One with whom we have to deal. He is the Lord of all.

So we said that Jesus came to earth to show man how to use this dominion legally. We'll look more at that in the next post. These are huge things to ponder. I have touched on some of these things in a previous post.

Dear Jesus, Help me to see and to ever be mindful of Your great plan for my life in this earth. Open my eyes to see wondrous things from Your word. I am ready to find You every day working on my behalf and I am ready to find the plan that You ordained for me from before the foundations of the world. I trust that Your plan is the best thing ever! I believe in that plan and I want to hear "Well done, thou good and faithful servant" when I see You face to face.~~May 1, 2021

NOTES

13. The Big Picture, Part 2

So in Part 1, we said that Jesus came to earth to show man how to legally use this dominion that God gave man from the very beginning.

Psalm 8:5 *For You have made him a little lower than the angels, And You have crowned him with glory and honor.* Most versions say "angels" in this passage, but the actual word used in the Hebrew language is "Elohim," which also translates as God or deities. I'm sure that can be debated, and is. Several translations show it as "a little lower than God." And the New Testament says in 1 Cor. 6:3 *"Do you not know that we shall judge angels? How much more, things that pertain to this life?"* Taking these two verses together, one could make the case for a translation of "God" in Psalm 8:5.

This elevation of man to just a bit lower than God Himself is HUUUGE. Man has a uniquely high position in the universe and in the mind of God. If we have been baptized in His Spirit, (Acts 1:4-5) we have access to His thoughts because of this indwelling Spirit of God. (1 Cor. 2) We are His temple, His home, the place He resides. We are now regenerated human beings.

The scriptures also say we are joint-heirs with Christ. There are some conditions attached to this in Romans 8:16-17. "*The Spirit Himself bears witness with our spirit that we are children of God, and if children, then heirs – heirs of God and joint heirs with Christ, if indeed we suffer with Him, that we may also be glorified together.*" When we are saved, we actually are placed in this position of heir-ship; we ARE heirs of God, but when an heir is a child, as we are at first, he is placed under guardianship until he matures and can actually inherit the full inheritance. (Galatians 4:1)

The suffering mentioned here implies several things. Romans 8:29 says, "*For whom He foreknew, He also predestined to be conformed to the image of His Son, that He might be the firstborn among many brethren.*" To be conformed to His image requires that we learn to think like God and love like God. Most of the time, our mind, will, and emotions get in the way of those goals. They have been trained by the world. Surrendering our own will and desires to His will and desires requires trusting Him implicitly, even when we don't understand what is going on.

I am reminded of a saying about the Israelites when they were set free from Egypt. It is said that God could take them out of Egypt, but He couldn't get Egypt out of them. They resisted transformation from their worldly ways. Egypt is a type of the world. We all have much of the world's ways and thinking in us that do not line up with the scriptures. Therefore, in order to get in agreement with God, we have to abandon those ways of thinking.

The Bible has this to say about that group in 1 Cor. 10:5-11 "*…with most of them God was not well pleased, for their bodies were scattered in the wilderness. Now these things became our examples, to the intent that we should not lust after evil things* *as they also lusted. And do not become idolaters as were some of them. As it is written, "The people sat down to eat and drink, and rose up to play." Nor let us commit sexual immorality, as some of them did, and in one day twenty-three thousand fell; nor let us tempt Christ, as some of them also tempted, and were destroyed by serpents; nor complain, as some of them also complained, and were destroyed by the destroyer. Now all these things happened to them as examples, and they were written for our admonition, upon whom the ends of the ages have come.*

God has given man dominion and rulership over satan, but in order to effectively function in that position, there is much about us that needs to change so that we can be trusted with that rulership. We start as newborn babies at salvation, but we are expected to learn from the Holy Spirit and be trained in the ways of God. Romans 12:2 says we are not to be conformed to this world, *"but be transformed by the renewing of your mind, that you may prove what is that good and acceptable and perfect will of God."*

This renewing is life long! Our training involves prayer, worship, study of the bible, church attendance, relationship with other believers and serving with the gifts God has given us. We are a part of the Body of Christ, which implies that we need other believers as part of our education and growth in the faith. And we need to learn to surrender always to God and His word as situations arise in our lives. We need to learn to deal with everything under His leadership, in the manner the Bible teaches us to behave. We are in school!

That is where the Israelites who left Egypt failed. They saw the wonderful rescue of God in the deliverance from the armies of Egypt at the Red Sea. They experienced the provision of food (manna) daily in the wilderness, the miraculous provision of water when they didn't have any, and more. When they refused to enter the Promised Land because of unbelief, they were set on a course to wander there for forty years. But miracles still happened. God provided for them; He took care of them. Their clothes and shoes never wore out for forty years, Deuteronomy 29:5 *"And I have led you forty years in the wilderness. Your clothes have not worn out on you, and your sandals have not worn out on your feet."* They saw miraculous things, but their *hearts* did not change. And that is why 1 Cor. 10 records what eventually happened to them. This is key.

When difficulty comes, what does your heart do? Grumble and complain? If so, you are not gaining ground in your life with God. But God still loves you. Or, do you ask God for answers to the problem? Do you pray? Do you search the scriptures to find out what He has to say on the matter? Do you take him aside as the disciples did in the gospels and humbly ask, "What is the meaning of this trial? What do I need to understand?"

The tests of life are just that: tests. Remember school? We take tests in order to gauge the level of our ability and to see if we qualify to move to the next grade. This is no different. The tests we take in life are for the same purpose. We need to learn to accept them, surrender to God in them, and find HIs purpose so that we can move on from there. I have found if I will do this, the trial is soon over.

James 1:2-4 *"My brethren, count it all joy when you fall into various trials, knowing that the testing of your faith produces patience. But let patience have its perfect work, that you may be perfect and complete, lacking nothing."* ~~ May 1, 2021

NOTES

14. Thirsting For God?

When I first got saved and filled with the Holy Spirit some 37 years ago, I had a hunger and thirst to know God that was practically UNquenchable! All I did at that time was go to my part time job, read the bible and pray. I devoured the New Testament probably five times in that first 6 months. I was HUNGRY and thirsty. I had so much to learn about Jesus.

Who was this Man who died to pay for my sins? Who was this Man who loved me that much? Did He really provide healing for my body too?

Later, I read books by other authors and listened to teachers on television. Their books I DRANK deeply from. Have you ever DRANK from a book? It's like cold fresh water from a well…it quenches your thirst.

Watchman Nee was a Chinese evangelist who was arrested and put in prison by the Chinese Communist Party in the early 50s after China's revolution. Before that, he had been a preacher/teacher to the Chinese people. He spent at least 20 years in a Chinese prison and died there in the early 1970s. But he wrote his sermons down and they were compiled into books that contain so much wisdom and faith, so much truth and so much nourishment for my soul. He dug deep and was a true expositor of the word of God. His writings are all in my library.

Another favorite teacher of mine was Myles Monroe. We discovered him in the early 90s on television. His messages on the original intent and purpose of God for man fed me too. These were things I had not heard anyone teach before. He died in a plane crash in this century and certainly far too early, as he and his wife were only in their 50s, but his books and recordings are still available and they are cherished at my home, laden with foundational truths I return to again and again to understand why I am here on the earth at this time.

Another writer/pastor I have drank deeply of is Francis Frangipane, who was originally pastor of a church in Cedar Rapids, Iowa. My husband and I have traveled several times to attend conferences at his church and have even met him in person. His books are also books to drink deeply from…timeless truths of the Kingdom of God and the ways of God. Francis taught us about becoming the image of Christ, which would provide a shelter from the works of darkness and was the intention of God in bringing His many sons into His own glory.

There are others who have been streams of still waters to drink from, but I would have to say these are at the top of the ticket. Today, I receive wonderful revelation from teacher Andrew Wommack, and Gary Keesee, who say things that add still more to my understanding of the Kingdom of God. Sometimes it is amazing what clarity one gets when someone says something just slightly differently than you have heard it before. Mazel Tov! (That means good luck has occurred!)

Lance Wallnau provides teaching, revelation and prophetic insight into the turbulent times we find ourselves in in our country today. The body of Christ needs leaders of integrity who can speak clearly as we navigate the troubled waters we find ourselves in. The Holy Spirit is in us and with us and points out things to us. We need teachers, prophets, apostles and the other gifts God has provided also. We are incomplete without them.

As Ephesians 4:11-14 says, "*And He Himself gave some to be apostles, some prophets, some evangelists, and some pastors and teachers, for the equipping of the saints for the work of ministry, for the edifying of the body of Christ, till we all come to the unity of the faith and of the knowledge of the Son of God, to a perfect man, to the measure of the stature of the fullness of Christ; that we should no longer be children, tossed to and fro and carried about with every wind of doctrine, by the trickery of men, in the cunning craftiness of deceitful plotting,...*" We are still in that process.

Are you thirsty for something you can't quite put your finger on? Does your life today satisfy you? If not, perhaps you need more of Jesus! ~~ May 1, 2021

NOTES

15. The Kingdom Way

I will first note that the ways of God and His Kingdom are not our ways. The bible even says so. We humans have been trained by the world's knowledge, which is vastly inferior to God's knowledge. God created everything we can see, touch, smell and hear, therefore He is vastly superior. The carnal mind is enmity against the ways of God. It cannot do otherwise. Romans 8:7 Because God knows everything, and sees everything, even the future, how can our human understanding possibly compete? We must acknowledge that he is far above mere humanity in wisdom, and is far more intelligent. We must accede to that. His wisdom knows no bounds. He is the most intelligent and knowledgeable Being in the universe.

As such, do you not think that knowing His ways and how He thinks would be something valuable to search out and follow so that your life can be a success? Isn't having a relationship with the Creator God who has such infinite qualities worth the effort? I have said this elsewhere, but I'll say it again… if I were to give you a very thick book and tell you that the person who wrote the book described great riches that belong to you, would you not search it out diligently to find out what those riches were? If you were given the last will and testament of a wealthy person and told that your name was in it and things of great value had been left for you, would you not search until you found what it was that person left for you?

That book, that will and testament, the bible, says that the fear of the Lord is the beginning of wisdom, not fear as in afraid, but fear as in reverence and honor. That book says to love the Lord your God with all your heart, your soul, your mind and your strength. First of all, before everything…He must be first. The thing that is created (we humans) must stay connected to the Creator. Just as a plant or a tree must stay connected to the dirt that it was made from (see Genesis 1 and 2), human beings, because they were created with a spirit, or breath from God, must stay connected to the Creator. If a tree or plant is disconnected from the dirt, we know what happens. They die.

So exactly what are God's ways?

In the gospels, we first see Jesus begin to say some strange things about God's ways in Matthew 5 in the Sermon on the Mount. Jesus began to teach the people about what the Kingdom of God was. He said: Blessed *are* the poor in spirit, For theirs is the kingdom of heaven; Blessed *are* those who mourn, For they shall be comforted; Blessed *are* the meek, For they shall inherit the earth (we do not see how the meek can inherit anything); Blessed *are* those who hunger and thirst for righteousness, For they shall be filled; Blessed *are* the merciful, For they shall obtain mercy; Blessed *are* the pure in heart, For they shall see God; Blessed *are* the peacemakers, For they shall be called sons of God; Blessed *are* those who are persecuted for righteousness' sake, For theirs is the kingdom of heaven (but no one likes persecution); Blessed are you when they revile and persecute you, and say all kinds of evil against you falsely for My sake (no one likes this either). Jesus said to rejoice and be exceedingly glad, for great *is* your reward in heaven, for so they persecuted the prophets who were before you.

Forgiving those who hurt you is the Kingdom way. We find forgiveness difficult because forgiving those who have hurt us is a divine attribute, not a human one. Jesus on the cross forgave those who were killing him. But God gives us the ability through HIs spirit to forgive others. Similar to this is praying for, and loving your enemies. Again, this is a divine attribute; we can only do it with His help. I remember a time that someone had offended me deeply and I was going to have to work in proximity with this person. My insides were fighting it. But I knew God wanted me to forgive her. As an act of my will, I said I would choose to forgive. And the Spirit of God removed all the bad feelings in my heart! It was amazing.

Jesus instructed the people, "*Do not worry about your life, what you will eat or what you will drink; nor about your body, what you will put on. Is not life more than food and the body more than clothing*?" Again, we will need divine help to accomplish this. The scripture goes on to say, "*Look at the birds of the air, for they neither sow nor reap nor gather into barns; yet your heavenly Father feeds them. Are you not of more value than they?*" We must believe that we are. Matthew 6:25-26

Giving away our money to worthy causes to extend God's Kingdom is the Kingdom way. Jesus said we are laying up treasures in Heaven when we do this. He said where your treasure is, there your heart will be. Giving money when you yourself have needs is the kingdom way. It is not a human attribute to give. We are selfish creatures.

Most things that God asks us to do make little sense to our minds.

Prayer is the Kingdom Way. We petition God for our needs and we trust Him when we have lack. We don't break man's law or God's commands in order to take care of our needs. He wants us to trust Him and see Him work on our behalf, believing that He is looking out for us

One teacher I know says fasting is the Kingdom way. Feasting on the Word of God instead of food and giving time to prayer is a Kingdom activity. I confess to not having a good understanding of fasting, but it was an activity of the Jewish people and the early church and is said to be an aid in increasing sensitivity to the Holy Spirit. Denying ourselves from anything we enjoy can be a spiritual discipline. We learn we don't have to have everything we want in order to be happy. We can allow our spirit to dominate our flesh and not allow ourselves to be cranky when we are deprived. Think of those who have suffered famine and hardship and imprisonment in far worse conditions than we have ever experienced.

Speaking words from the bible in our prayers and decrees is the Kingdom Way. Jesus told his disciples to pray this way: "*Thy kingdom come, Thy will be done on earth as it is in Heaven.*" Our words have power. "*Death and life are in the power of the tongue and those who love it will eat its fruit.*" Proverbs 18:21 Speaking words is the Kingdom Way. God created the world with words. We are made in the image and likeness of God, therefore, we also create with words, for good or for evil. James 3:6 says "*the tongue is a fire, a world of iniquity. The tongue is so set among our members that it defiles the whole body, and sets on fire the course of nature; and it is set on fire by hell."* The tongue is powerful indeed.

Dear Jesus, We are not trained in Your ways. Your ways are so foreign to us. We must have Your light and Your understanding to even begin to see the value of closely following after You. We desperately need to see Your plan for our lives so that we can fulfill Your will in the earth. Teach us Your ways. We want to see Your Kingdom come.-~~June 11, 2021

NOTES

16. In The Beginning, Now and Forever

In the beginning, Adam and Eve walked and talked with God. They had a relationship with Him.

In the New Testament, Jesus said eternal life is knowing God and Jesus Christ. John 17:3. Our life here on earth is about eternal life. I have always thought (and I think most people do) that eternal life just meant living forever, but Jesus defined eternal life as something much more. Shortly before His death, He prayed in John 17:1-3, *"Father, the hour has come. Glorify Your Son, that He may also glorify You, as You have given Him authority over all flesh, that You may give eternal life to as many as You have given Him., And this is eternal life, that they might know You, the only true God, and Jesus Christ whom you have sent."*

If we go back to the Garden of Eden, we see God barring access to the tree of Life from Adam and Eve, "lest they eat of it and stay in their sinful condition forever." Our compact with God now provides the right to "eat" of "the tree of Life" (which is Jesus, Who is the source of all true spiritual knowledge) because redemption from our sins has been paid for and we have received it. We can now *"come boldly to the throne of grace to receive mercy in time of need."* (Hebrews 10) The way to know God has been fully opened to us.

God is working to bring us back to the one goal that should be our single aim in life around which everything else revolves, including our choice of marriage partners, our careers, where we should live, every decision....it's all about Him! Ephesians 2:20 "*For we are His workmanship, created in Christ Jesus for good works, which God prepared beforehand that we should walk in them.*" "*All things are to be summed up in Him, things in Heaven and things upon the earth.*" Ephesians 1:10. Jeremiah 1:5 points to the fact that we are each here for a specific purpose that God has planned. "*Before I formed you in the womb I knew you; Before you were born I sanctified you; I ordained you a prophet to the nations.*"

It truly is all about Him. He is the Judge of mankind. All judgment has been given to Jesus Christ; the Father now judges no one because of His sacrifice. John 5:22-23

It took 4000 years to get Jesus born into the earth through a woman "*in the fullness of time.*" Galatians 4:14 All throughout the Old Testament, men worshipped God. After Noah preached for 100 years while building the ark, the flood came and wiped all mankind off the earth, except for the eight people in the ark. The first thing Noah did after he was able to embark was to worship God, to build an altar and worship Him. And at that, God promised never to destroy the earth with a flood again. At the end of Genesis chapter 4, we see that men began to call upon the name of the Lord.

Not all men after that worshipped, but all throughout Old Testament history, there were men who sought God, talked to God, heard from God, got direction from Him and fought battles and won them in His name. Man's understanding is limited whereas God's mind is infinite. We come from Him, we are like Him, we are regenerated human beings if we are saved and filled with His Spirit, but we are not Him. He is still the boss by virtue of being the Creator. It's better to learn that lesson early in life.

In the book of Revelation, again we see worship going on into eternity. The outpouring of the love of the redeemed of the Lord will never be spent, never satiated, will never burn out as they continually give expression to the fact that Someone loved them enough to rescue them from sin, destruction and the devil, by taking the death penalty they themselves deserved. Once a person understands that, they can only worship the Lamb Who sits on the throne.

Hallelujah. We love You forever, Lord Jesus.~~June 23, 2021

NOTES

17. Why We Are Where We Are

I've been listening lately to some exceptional teaching about the way believers lose their confidence before God by listening to a sin conscience. Andrew Wommack teaches how a conscience of sin actually makes believers lose their confidence before God and weakens their faith. They are then subject to the works of darkness. They have been deceived.

Wommack believes most of the church actually still functions in this manner with weakened faith because of a sin conscience. I think I agree with that. I think most failures of faith and therefore our Christian living, can be attributed to this reason. There may be other reasons for what we see in our society today, but I think this may be the biggest reason for the church's failure to impress and impact the culture, thereby leading to the tsunami of darkness we are seeing our nation come under.

I have been a part of the full gospel Spirit-filled church for 37 years now and have attended various church groups, as well as some denominational groups. I have seen lots of sin and failure, with local pastors falling into sin and being exposed. It is devastating to the advancement of God's message to the culture. Any amount of performance-based legalism taught in the church will produce sin and failure of faith in our lives. Too many succumb to the condemnation of the evil one and cannot arise from it. I have my own experiences with a conscience of sin in my earlier years of learning how to walk in faith.

The truth is, no matter what a believer does, God still loves them, forgives them and works with them. They are not condemned to hell or even to second-class status because of something they did. God's ACCEPTANCE of us is not based on what we DO…think about that, because most people cannot understand it. The human mind cannot grasp it. See my previous article here. When we sin, it is because we do not really, deeply, grasp what Jesus did for us, how he freed us and gave us His righteousness. We don't totally understand the position and the condition He has elevated us to.

God's acceptance of us is simply based on what Jesus DID. If we are born again, God is pleased with us BEFORE we ever do anything for Him. He loved us BEFORE we loved Him. Probably the greatest Old Testament example of this is King David. David sinned greatly by committing adultery with Bathsheba and setting up her husband to be killed in battle to cover Bathsheba's pregnancy. In my opinion, there is almost nothing that could be worse than all of that! But we don't see God abandoning David. We see a prophet coming to him to let him know of his sin and we see David and his family experiencing consequences from this situation, but we also see redemption in the fact that another child from Bathsheba became the successor king to David. The point is, God did not abandon David, who wrote much of the Book of Psalms, documenting his prayers and relationship with God. In 2 Samuel 12:13, we see David obtaining forgiveness from the God he loved.

"So David said to Nathan, "I have sinned against the LORD." And

Nathan said to David, "THE LORD ALSO HAS PUT AWAY YOUR SIN (emphasis mine); you shall not die. However, because by this deed you have given great occasion to the enemies of the LORD to blaspheme, the child also who is born to you shall surely die."

This sin conscience weakness in the church will not allow us to confront the works of darkness in our society because we do not have the confidence in God to do so. Instead, we have self-doubt. This must change if we are to be successful in confronting the darkness we see taking over our nation. We must have warriors with the confidence to do spiritual battle. Witness the same David as a 17 year old who saw the armies of Israel quaking before the giant Goliath. These men who had been trained for war certainly had no confidence before the tall giant Goliath. The 17 year old David who only showed up to bring lunch to his army brothers looked at the situation and said, "Who is this uncircumcised Philistine to defy the armies of the living God?" David then killed that giant and cut off his head with Goliath's own sword. How was he able to do this? David wasn't looking at his own weaknesses; he was looking at his God. He was strong in faith. He wasn't looking at his own youth or inexperience.

Now that is confidence. That's how it's done. That's what the church must do in the spirit. We don't kill people, but we do deal with the demonic forces that are motivating people. Goliath is representative of the invisible demonic powers that oppose all that is good and decent in this world. Jesus waits for us to make the devil His footstool. *The devil has already been defeated by Him*. I want to say that louder. THE DEVIL HAS ALREADY BEEN DEFEATED BY JESUS! But we, the church, are to enforce His victory! He has given us everything we need to "make it so." His sacrifice made us perfect forever! We can be supremely confidant in the abilities our God has given us! Take His word as TRUTH and use it.

Hebrews 10:12-14 "*But this Man, after He had offered one sacrifice for sins forever, sat down at the right hand of God, from that time waiting till His enemies are made His footstool. For by one offering He has perfected forever those who are being sanctified.*"~~ July 17, 2021

NOTES

18. Are God's Love and God's Approval the Same Thing?

In my previous post, I talked about how God loves us and that His acceptance of us is not based on our performance. I feel the need to discuss these two words, love and acceptance, because I believe there is much confusion in our society today about this. We hear such things as, if you love me, you will accept my lifestyle, my choices.

So let's talk about this.

God LOVES everyone. John 3:16 "*For God so loved the world (that includes everyone) that He gave His only begotten Son, that whosoever believes in Him should not perish, but have eternal life.*"

John 3:17 "*For God did not send His Son into the world to condemn the world, but that the world through Him might be saved.*"

So because God LOVED everyone in the world, He sent His Son Jesus to live a holy sinless life, and then give HIs life on the cross as the sacrifice for all the sins ever committed and all the sins that will be committed by everyone, forever. According to John 3:17, God did not send HIs Son into the world to condemn us. God's love encompasses all and is FOR all. He has left NO ONE out of this invitation. All are invited to come to Him and accept this sacrifice that He gave for all peoples.

As parents, do we not love ALL of our children, just based on the fact they are our children? Of course we do!

So, for those who choose to accept that sacrifice for the payment of their sins, the way is now open for those to come boldly before the "throne of grace." Hebrews 4:16. They now have God's favor and pleasure, before they ever did a thing for Him. The sin barrier has been removed. God is pleased with their actions.

For example, you have children. One of them does good things, lives a good life, raises his children, and works hard for his family. The family prospers; things are good. What more could a parent ask for but that their children have good, healthy, prosperous lives? Does the parent love this child who does good? Of course he does.

Another child lives a life of indolence, may do drugs, abandons his children and family, and breaks the law. This one may even go to prison for crimes, but this child is not living a life that will prosper. Does the parent love this child? Of course he does!

But the parent disagrees with, or hates, the choices this child has made. He grieves for this child, but his love is definitely still there. He hates the fact that this child is not prospering in his life, but he still loves him. His disapproval is only based on lifestyle choices, not on the child himself. A parent can see the outcome of this child's choice will not be good and, if he is a normal parent, he wishes to save that child the pain that is surely coming.

LOVING A PERSON DOES NOT EQUAL ACCEPTANCE OF THEIR LIFE CHOICES. This is what society is so messed up about right now. People are equating non-acceptance of their lifestyle choices with hating. This is simply not true. It is a lie of satan and those people are deceived. The Christian is commanded in scripture to love, but we are not commanded to accept every screwball idea that comes down the track! We would be dishonest if we did that and doing no one any favors.

And so to continue, God loves everyone, but just like a parent, He does not accept or agree with all of people's lifestyle choices. Want to know why?

Because there are extremely painful consequences to those choices that fall under the domain of evil. You may not believe in evil, or the devil, but your unbelief in it doesn't make it not true. I suggest you read the book of truth, the bible, and you will find out. Of course, if you are reading this post, you most likely already read the bible.

God loves us enough that He wants us to avoid the extremely painful consequences of bad choices, just like any good parent does. The book of truth, the bible, is full of stories of the lives of those who chose good, and those chose evil. The outcomes of their lives is written there for all to learn from. And if you are really paying attention, look to the lives of those around you. Who is having good come in their life? Who is not?

Which outcome do you want for your life? ~~ July 17, 2021

NOTES

19. Is God Hindered By Our Unbelief?

Most of us would say that God can do anything. He is sovereign. Most of us would say we believe that.

But I would like to challenge that on some level...God didn't stop Adam and Eve from eating of the tree of the knowledge of Good and Evil. Why not? He gave them free will to make a choice. We are not robots. So was God sovereign then? (I would argue yes, he still was sovereign and knew that they would make that choice and had already made a provision for sin in Jesus.)

In Matthew 13 and Mark 6:5, there is the story of when Jesus went to his hometown. This story is rather fascinating if one is looking at the sovereignty of God. Speaking of Jesus, the scriptures say *"Now He could do no mighty work there, except that He laid His hands on a few sick people and healed them."* There are other stories in the bible that could be looked at.

These events indicate God's desires and plans are hindered by decisions men make and the condition of men's hearts. The great Old Testament city of Nineveh was saved at the preaching of a reluctant prophet named Jonah who didn't even want to be there, but who finally made it after a detour.

But 100 years later, the city fell into such depravity again that it was destroyed.

Men can either live in the realm of darkness where demonic powers control him, or man can live in the light, where God's truth is. It's always man's choice. But I believe God is always trying to bring man to the light. That is His desire.

The children of Israel were brought out of Egypt in a mighty display of God's delivering power, crossed the Red Sea on dry ground with Pharaoh's forces coming in behind them, then saw the waters close in on the Egyptian forces. They saw wonderful acts of God's power to feed them and give them water when they needed it, keep clothes and shoes on them for 40 years, but yet Hebrews Chapter 4 has this to say about them:

"Let us therefore fear, lest, a promise being left us of entering into his rest, any of you should seem to come short of it. For unto us was the gospel preached, as well as unto them: ***but the word preached did not profit them, not being mixed with faith*** *in them that heard it."*

God gave them every reason to believe in and trust Him, yet they did not. We should not miss the times of our visitation when God is speaking to us or showing us things. We need to pay attention.

Psalm 103:9 says that God "will not strive with us forever...." That means there is an end point in a person's life as well as an end point in the history of the earth when "*in the dispensation of the fullness of the times He might gather together in one all things in Christ, both which are in heaven and which are on earth – in Him."* Ephesians 1:10.

It is God's will, His desire, that all men be saved and come to the knowledge of the truth, but yet we see that all men do not choose Him. Why not? It is God's will, His desire, but yet men have the choice to reject Him and His ways.

God does not always get His way, it would appear, perhaps in the short term. God does not want people to be separated from Him forever in hell. But mankind is still definitely on the way to a destination that is prophesied in the bible, where Jesus is "*waiting till His enemies are made His footstool.*" Hebrews 10:13. That IS going to happen. Let us keep looking up, look for and even hasten the day of His coming as we grow in holy living.

2 Peter 3:11-12 "*Therefore, since all these things will be dissolved, what manner of persons ought you to be in holy conduct and godliness, looking for and hastening the coming of the day of God, because of which the heavens will be dissolved, being on fire, and the elements will melt with fervent heat?* ~~ July 17, 2021

NOTES

20. The Kingdom Suffers Violence

Matthew 11:11-13 *"Verily I say unto you, Among them that are born of women there has not risen a greater than John the Baptist: notwithstanding he that is least in the kingdom of heaven is greater than he. And from the days of John the Baptist until now the kingdom of heaven suffers violence, and the violent take it by force. For all the prophets and the law prophesied until John…*

This passage of scripture has always been a bit intriguing to me. What could it possibly mean? What does it mean the kingdom of heaven suffers violence? Other scriptures tell us to ask, seek and knock and keep it up. Don't quit.

I would like to submit to you some examples from the scriptures where we see people absolutely committed to not giving up on what they want from God. The New Testament has several instances where people pestered Jesus with this attitude.

There is one Old Testament example I am thinking of and that is Daniel. In Daniel chapter 10, we see Daniel staying in a posture of prayer and fasting for a full three weeks before the angel could break through the heavenly battle to get the answer to him. What would have happened if Daniel had not stayed at it for three weeks? Would he have received his answer?

In the New Testament, I am first reminded of the story of the Syrophoenician woman who absolutely would not take no for an answer from Jesus, even though He tried to dissuade her. Matthew 15:21-28, Mark 7:24-30. She had no right to Israel's benefits. She had no covenant with God and was therefore outside of the benefits that God bestows. But Jesus gave in to her and commended her faith. It is a remarkable story.

Another story that Jesus told was the one about the woman pestering the judge until he gave her what she wanted. Luke 18:1-8. She refused to quit.

Blind Bartimaeus in Mark 10:46-52 was not dissuaded by those around him who told him to shut up while he was crying out for Jesus's attention. He got his eyes healed.

The woman with the issue of blood had spent all her money for 14 years with no cure in sight. She pressed through the crowd to get what she wanted even though she was unclean and could have been stoned to death for it. Matthew 9:20-22, Mark 5:25-34, Luke 8:43-48. She was healed.

Jesus sent out the seventy disciples to cast out devils and heal the sick. They came back rejoicing that the demons were subject to them, which was really GREAT news! Jesus told them He saw satan fall like lightning from Heaven and to rejoice not so much about that, but to rejoice that their names were written in Heaven. Luke 10:17-20. I believe Jesus was referring to seeing demonic powers lose their grip on the people the disciples had ministered to.

When God's people go out and preach the Good News, healing the sick and casting out demons, the immediate heavens do suffer loss and great confusion comes to the demonic powers. They lose their authority over men when that truth is preached. They hate the blood of Jesus that was shed for us and they hate it that they got beat at the cross. There is also more "violence' that Heaven suffers as men learn the truth that salvation includes healing for their bodies, that their needs are provided for, and that God has a plan for their lives that they can find out. The postures of standing, insisting, claiming and pounding on the door as we see in some of the examples cited above, is required to obtain most of God's promises. I suspect that many are ignorant of this fact, relying on the sovereignty of God to provide their needs, (the thinking, "well whatever God wills") or, they give up too soon before seeing the answer to their petitions. Some do not have the confidence in their right standing with God to take this stance and to insist on receiving from Heaven. They may take a posture of begging God instead. These are never quite sure that it really belongs to them.

Our right standing with God was only provided through acceptance of Jesus's payment for our sins. This alone restores our relationship to God. There is nothing we did to earn it in any fashion. It is strictly based on what Jesus did on the cross.

In this great exchange, our sin for His righteousness, God has given us salvation, healing, and provision. It's in "the will", or the New Testament. If you were to read someone's will and find out they left you a million dollars, would you not insist on getting it? Would you not say "That is rightfully mine and

I want it?" We need to ascertain what the "will" of God is and then go after it until we see it manifested in our world. Heaven is waiting and the devil will try to stop it because that's his job. He hates God and he hates you. Our job is see the kingdom come and to enforce the will of God in the earth that Jesus has already proclaimed and died to provide. That's why we pray, "Thy kingdom come, Thy will be done" as we are instructed in Matthew 6:10. The New Testament declares what the will of God is.

Let us not delay!

Hebrews 3:14-15 "*For we have become partakers of Christ if we hold the beginning of our confidence steadfast to the end, while it is said: "Today, if you will hear His voice, Do not harden your hearts as in the rebellion.*"~~ July 27, 2021

NOTES

21. Everything Summed Up in Christ

Ephesians 1:9-10 says this: "*…having made known to us the mystery of His will, according to His good pleasure which He purposed in Himself, that in the dispensation of the fullness of the times He might gather together in one all things in Christ, both which are in heaven and which are on earth – in Him.*

What does this verse mean? Let's look at different versions of it to gain understanding. This is said to be the goal of history by some.

"*he made known to us the mystery of his will according to his good pleasure, which he purposed in Christ, to be put into effect when the times reach their fulfillment – to bring unity to all things in heaven and on earth under Christ*" NIV
"*God has now revealed to us his mysterious will regarding Christ – which is to fulfill his own good plan. And this is the plan: At the right time he will bring everything together under the authority of Christ – everything in heaven and on earth.*" New Living Translation
"*He made known to us the mystery of His will according to His good pleasure, which He purposed in Christ, with regard to the fulfillment of the times [that is, the end of history, the climax of the ages]–to bring all things together in Christ, [both] things in the heavens and things on the earth.*" Amplified Bible

"God did what he had purposed, and made known to us the secret plan he had already decided to complete by means of Christ. This plan, which God will complete when the time is right, is to bring all creation together, everything in heaven and on earth, with Christ as head." God's Word Translation

This verse speaks of God's goal that all things in creation are to be brought back into order. I maintain that also means that God's created human race is to be brought into order. And that means that those of us who believe concede to letting God bring US back into order, in our attitudes, our choices, and our relationships with others.

The pressures of life are there to "press" us into conformity to the character and nature of Jesus. Every "press" that brings a negative reaction is a place where Jesus needs to be manifested. We were given His nature when we were saved, but we have old habits and ways of thinking that are not of the Kingdom. They are not of God and so we must be transformed and changed. We are automatically changed inside and given a new nature when we are saved, but we must also *"work out our own salvation, with fear and trembling"* (Phil. 2:12) and *"and be not conformed to this world: but be transformed by the renewing of your mind, that you may prove what is that good, and acceptable, and perfect, will of God."* (Romans 12:2)

God has a plan, a desire, a will for each of us that all fits into His BIG plan for the world, The human mind is unable to fathom this for 7.6 billion people currently inhabiting the earth plus all of those who have gone before and all of those to come. But it's true, He does have something for each of us to do, a part to play in His Grand Scheme of Things. He knows all of us intimately and why we were brought to the earth. We all get a choice whether to play that part or not. And

I have observed in my own life that God is able to move people around, just by a desire one may have in one's heart. You don't even know that's what is happening.

We can look at Bible stories and see the people who obeyed God and the people who didn't obey God. They didn't agree to the plan. Abraham went out not knowing where he was going when God told him to leave his homeland. Jonah on the other hand, refused to go to Ninevah and give those ungodly people a chance to repent and turn to God. Then look what happened to him. He took a detour, but ended up being somewhat agreeable to what God asked him to do, after he suffered the consequences. I call him the reluctant prophet, as he seemed to still be mad about it all even after the city turned from wickedness.

Daniel submitted to ungodly wicked kings in captivity in Babylon, being faithful to God and receiving great revelations about what would happen in the end times of the world. He discovered the prophecy from Jeremiah about the captivity being close to an end and became a part of bringing it to pass with his prayers and fasting.

Esther in captivity obeyed when her people were under threat of extinction and saved them by her obedience and faithfulness. She saved the nation from whom our Savior Jesus would come. Rahab the prostitute assisted the Israelites at Jericho and came into the direct lineage of Jesus. Do not discount your littleness. These all felt the pressure and came into God's plan for that time.

So I think we can agree that all things are moving toward a distinct destination, or plan, that God has in His mind. There is a culmination of things coming. We are all being moved in that direction. Those who are not saved are feeling the pressure and seeking ways out of it, through drugs, alcohol, sex, shopping, whatever it might be that relieves their pressure. Those of us who are saved and are disciples of Jesus are however, looking in a different direction. We are looking up, knowing the time of our redemption is drawing near. But it is also a time when the ungodly may begin to look up, as a time of reformation and salvation is coming for them too. That is God's will, God's plan. Let us be ready! Let every man "*be ready to give an answer for the hope that is in him*" to those who do not know Him yet. 1 Peter 3:15. "*Always be ready to give a defense to everyone who asks you a reason for the hope that is in you, with meekness and fear;*"

We too feel the pressure. But we are, or ought to be, turning to Jesus for the answers. He has a way for us to deal with things and it is not as the world deals with things! This is how all things are summed up in Him. Every time we turn to Him when the pressure comes, and submit to His plan, we win and He wins! The Kingdom wins. We are being conformed to His likeness and fulfilling His plan to sum up all things, even things about ourselves, in Christ. Everything is being brought into conformity with Him, is another way to say it. He is waiting until His enemies become His footstool. His plan is that we carry the nature and life of Jesus. The plan is for us to live like Jesus lived and do the things He did. And even greater things are planned for us. We are to be sons and daughters who bring Him glory and that is how we do it, by submitting to His plan and His desires. We are not to be like Jonah, suspicious and harboring ill will toward God and hating the ungodly so much that we don't want to share salvation with them. Oh, let it never be!

We are to love people like He loves people, and think towards them like He thinks. The more we practice this, the more the attributes of Heaven that will come to us, and the higher our rewards in Heaven will be. We haven't even talked about that!

But yes, there are rewards in Heaven for how much we submitted to Him here on earth. Of course all of our rewards and crowns will be cast at His feet because we could never, ever have done it without Him! Never! We could never be good on our own, we could never love people on our own. It's all because of Him! He deserves all the praise and glory for it all.

"For by Him all things were created that are in heaven and that are on earth, visible and invisible, whether thrones or dominions or principalities or powers. All things were created through Him and for Him. And He is before all things, and in Him all things consist. And He is the head of the body, the church, who is the beginning, the firstborn from the dead, that in all things He may have the preeminence. For it pleased the Father that in Him all the fullness should dwell, and by Him to reconcile all things to Himself, by Him, whether things on earth or things in heaven, having made peace through the blood of His cross." Colossians 1:16-20 ~~ August 5, 2021

NOTES

Katherine Sands is a freelance writer and artist who is currently working as the editor of a local newspaper and website. She has been published in a national magazine and is the author of the first two Dogtags and Pearls books and the author of three children's books: A Tale of Two Lambs. The ABCs of Created Things, and A Tale of Two Prophets. She also illustrated the last two children's books.

Katherine and her husband David reside in Carmi, Ill.

www.ingramcontent.com/pod-product-compliance
Lightning Source LLC
LaVergne TN
LVHW012114160826
845678LV00014B/3095

* 9 7 9 8 5 4 9 1 8 2 5 4 7 *